WOMAN
AND WAR

FROM
"WOMAN AND LABOR"

BY

OLIVE SCHREINER

British Library Cataloguing-in-Publication Data
A catalogue record for this book is available from
the British Library

Olive Schreiner

Olive Emilie Albertina Schreiner was born on 24th March 1855 at the Wesleyan Missionary Society station at Wittebergen in the Eastern Cape, near Herschel in South Africa. She was the ninth of twelve children born to Gottlob Schreiner and Rebecca Lyndall, who both worked as Christian missionaries.

Olive's early education was provided by her mother, who was both well read and gifted. She aimed to teach her children the same restraint and self-discipline that had been part of her own upbringing. Her father, however, was not such a capable man and although loving an gentle, failed in many of the pursuits he engaged in causing the family to live in abject poverty much of the time.

Upon completing her later formal education, Olive chose to become a governess, taking her first post at Barkly East. At this time she became increasingly disillusioned with the religion of her parents and siblings, a subject on which they would have many arguments. When a friend lent her a copy of Herbert Spencer's *First Principles*, it had a profound impact on her and helped develop her ideas of a morality free of organised religion.

In 1880, Olive set sail for the United Kingdom with the goal of taking a position as a trainee nurse at the Royal Infirmary in Edinburgh in Scotland. Unfortunately ill-health prevented her from studying and she was forced to concede that writing would and could be her only work in life. In 1883, she produced her first published work *The Story of an African Farm* which she penned under the pseudonym Ralph Iron. This novel details the lives of three characters, first as children and then as adults, and caused significant controversy over its frank portrayal of freethought, feminism, premarital sex, and transvestitism. She left England in 1886 for mainland Europe where she was tremendously productive, writing numerous allegories and even working on an introduction to Mary Wollstonecraft's *A Vindication of the Rights of Women*.

She returned to South Africa in 1889 and became increasingly involved with the politics of the area, leading her to make influential acquaintances such as Cecil John Rhodes, with whom she eventually became disillusioned and wrote a scathing allegory in his honour.

In 1894, she married a politically active farmer, Samuel Cronwright. They had one child together that died after just one day. This was followed by numerous pregnancies, all of which ended in miscarriages.

Olive Schreiner remained politically active through continuous ill-health with asthma and angina, and while in England receiving treatment, was even in contact with Ghandi and other prominent activists of the pacifist movement. She died in South Africa on 11th December 1920 and was buried in Kimberly. Following Samuel Cronwright's death, Olive's body was exhumed and laid to rest along with her baby, dog and husband at the top of Buffelskop mountain, on the farm known as Buffelshoek, near Cradock, in the Eastern Cape.

FOREWORD

No excuse is needed for reprinting at this time from Olive Schreiner's classic, "WOMAN AND LABOR," her treatment of "Woman and War." There is no other exposition of women's natural hatred of war so searching, so true and so moving as this. Her inspired words on the subject, beyond their importance as a deeply significant statement of the attitude of women toward bloodshed and killing, to be read and taken to heart in its bearing on the greatest war in history, are vital as a prophecy of how war in the future will pass away.

It is a curious fact that the whole

fate of the book, "WOMAN AND LABOR," is connected with war. In the introduction the author tells of the irreparable destruction of the nearly completed manuscript of which the book as published is but a reminiscent fragment. She had finally finished, she tells us, the work on women which had occupied a large part of her life since her early youth. There only remained revision and the writing of a preface before publication. She continues the story thus:

"In 1899 I was living in Johannesburg, when, owing to ill-health, I was ordered suddenly to spend some time at a lower level. At the end of two months the Boer War broke out. Two days after war was proclaimed I arrived at De Aar on my way back to the Transvaal; but martial law had already been proclaimed there, and the military authorities refused to allow me to return to my home in the Transvaal and sent me down to the Colony; nor was I allowed to send any communication through, to any person who might have extended some care over my possessions. Some eight months after, when the British troops had taken and entered Johannesburg, a friend, who, being on the British side, had been allowed to go up, wrote me that he had visited my house and found it looted and that all that was of value had been taken or destroyed; my desk had been forced open and broken up, and its contents set on fire in the center of the room, so that the roof was blackened over the pile of burnt papers. He added that there was little in the remnants of paper of which I could make any use, but that he had gathered and stored the fragments till such time as I might be allowed to come and see them. I thus knew my book had been destroyed.

"Some months later in the war when confined in a little up-country hamlet many hundreds of miles from the coast and from Johannesburg; with the brunt of the war at that time breaking round us, de Wet was said to have crossed the Orange River and to have been within a few miles of us, and the British columns moved hither and thither. I was living in a little house on the outskirts of the village, in a single room, with a stretcher and two packing-cases as furniture, and with only my little dog for company. Thirty-six armed African natives were set to guard night and day at the doors and windows of the house;

and I was only allowed to go out during certain hours in the middle of the day to fetch water from the fountain in the middle of the village, or to buy what I needed. I was allowed to receive no newspapers or magazines.

"A high barbed wire fence, guarded by armed natives, surrounded the village, through which it would have been death to try to escape. All day the pom-poms from the armored trains that paraded on the railway line nine miles distant could be heard at intervals; and at night there was the talk of the armed natives as they pressed against the windows, and the tramp of the watch with the endless "Who goes there?" as they walked round the wire fence through the long, dark hours when I was neither allowed to light a candle nor strike a match. When a conflict was fought near by, the dying and wounded were brought in; three men belonging to our little village were led out to execution; death sentences were read in our little market-place; our prison was filled with our fellow-countrymen; and we did not know from hour to hour what the next would bring to us.

"Under these conditions I felt it necessary I should resolutely force my thought at times from the horror of the world around me, to dwell on some abstract question, and it was under these circumstances that this little book was written, being a remembrance mainly drawn from one chapter of the larger book. The armed native guards standing against the windows, it was impossible to open the shutters, and the room was therefore so dark that even the physical act of writing was difficult.

"A year and a half after, when the war was over and peace had been proclaimed for about four months, I with difficulty obtained a permit to visit the Transvaal. I found among the burnt fragments the leathern back of my book intact, but the front half of the leaves had been completely burnt away; the back half of the leaves next to the cover were still all there, but so browned and scorched with the flames that they broke as you touched them; and there was nothing left but to destroy it. I even then had a hope that at some future time I might yet rewrite the whole book. But life is short; and I have found that not only shall I never rewrite the book, but I shall not have the health even to fill out and harmonize this little remembrance from it.

"It is with some pain that I give out this fragment. I am only comforted by the thought that perhaps all sincere and earnest search after truth, even where it fails to reach it, yet often comes so near to it that other minds more happily situated may be led, by pointing out its very limitations, to obtain a larger view."

WOMAN AND WAR

I

IT may be said, "Granting fully that you are right, that, as woman's old fields of labor slip from her, she must grasp new, or must become wholly dependent on her sexual function alone, all the other elements of human nature in her becoming atrophied and arrested through lack of exercise, and granting that her evolution being arrested, the evolution of the whole race will be also arrested in her person; granting all this to the full, and allowing that the bulk of human labor tends to become more and more intellectual and less and less purely mechanical as perfected machinery takes the place of crude human exertion; and that therefore if woman is to be saved from degeneration and parasitism, and the body of humanity from arrest, she must receive a training which will cultivate all the intellectual and all the physical faculties and be allowed freely to employ them; nevertheless, would it not be possible, and be well, that a dividing line of some kind should be drawn between the occupations of men and of women? Would it not be possible that woman should retain agriculture, textile manufactory, trade, domestic management, the education of youth, and medicine, in addition to child-bearing, as her exclusive fields of toil; while to the male should be left the study of abstract science, law and war, and statecraft; as of old, man took war and the chase, and woman absorbed the further labors of life? Why should there not be again a fair and even division in the field of social labor?"

Superficially, this suggestion appears rational, having at least this to recommend it, that it appears to harmonize with the course of human evolution in the past; but closely examined, it will, we think, be found to have no practical or scientific basis, and to be out of harmony with the conditions of modern life. In ancient and primitive societies, the mere larger size and muscular strength of man in certain mechanical directions, and woman's incessant physical activity in child-bearing and suckling, made almost inevitable such a sexual division of labor in almost all coun-

tries, save perhaps in ancient Egypt.[1]
Woman naturally took the heavy agri-
cultural and domestic labors, which
were yet more consistent with the con-
tinual dependence of infant life on her
own, than those of man in war and the
chase. There was nothing artificial in
such a division; it threw the heaviest
burden of the most wearying and unex-
citing forms of social labor on woman,
but under it both sexes labored, and
each transmitted to the other, through
inheritance, the fruit of its slowly ex-
panding and always exerted powers;
and the race progressed.

Individual women might sometimes,

---

[1] The division of labor between the sexes in
ancient Egypt and other exceptional countries is
a matter of much interest, which cannot here be
entered on.

and even often, become the warriors or chiefs of tribes; the King of Ashantee might train his terrible regiment of females; and men might now and again plant and weave for their children: but in the main, and in most societies, the division of labor was just, natural, beneficial, and it was inevitable that such a division should take place. Were to-day a band of civilized men, women, and infants thrown down absolutely naked and defenseless in some desert, and cut off hopelessly from all external civilized life, undoubtedly very much the old division of labor would, at least for a time, reassert itself. Men would look about for stones and sticks with which to make weapons, with which to repel wild beasts and enemies, and would go a-hunting meat and tend the

[17]

beasts when tamed;[1] women would suckle their children, cook the meat men brought, build shelters, look for roots and if possible cultivate them. There certainly would be no parasite in the society. The woman who refused to labor for her offspring, and the man who refused to hunt or defend society would not be supported by their fellows, would soon be extinguished by want. As wild beasts were extinguished and others tamed and the materials for war improved, fewer men would be needed for hunting and war; then they would remain at home and aid in building and planting; many women would retire into the house to perfect domestic toil and handicrafts, and on a small scale the common an-

[1] The young captured animals would probably be tamed and reared by the women.

cient evolution of society would practically repeat itself. But for the present we see no such natural and sponta-
neous division of labor based on natural
sexual distinctions in the new fields of
intellectual or delicately skilled man-
ual labor, which are taking the place
of the old.

II

It is possible, though at present there is nothing to give indication of such a fact, and it seems highly improbable, that, in some subtle manner now incomprehensible, there might tend to be a subtle correlation between that condition of the brain and nervous system which accompanies ability in the direction of certain forms of mental, social labor and the particular form of reproductive function possessed by an individual. It may be that, inexplicable as it seems, there may ultimately be found to be some connection between that condition of the brain and nervous system which fits the individual for the study of the higher mathematics, let us say, and the nature of their sex attributes. The mere fact that, of the handful of women who, up to the present, have received training and been allowed to devote themselves to abstract study, several have excelled in the higher mathematics, proves of necessity no preëminent tendency on the part of the female sex in the direction of mathematics, as compared to labor in the fields of statesmanship, administration, or law, as into these fields there has been practically no admittance for women. It is sometimes stated, that as several women of genius in modern times have sought to find expression for their creative powers in the art of fiction, there must be some inherent connection in the human brain between the ovarian sex function and the art of fiction. The fact is that modern fiction, being merely a description of human life in any of its phases, and being the only art that can be exercised without special training or special appliances, and produced in the moments stolen from the multifarious, brain-destroying occupations which fill the average woman's life, they have been driven to find this outlet for their powers as the only one presenting itself. How far otherwise might have been the directions in which their genius would naturally have expressed itself can be known only to the women themselves; what the world has lost by that compulsory expression of genius, in a form which may not have been its most natural form of expression, or only one of its forms, no one can ever know. Even in the little third-rate novelist whose works cumber the ground, we see often a pathetic figure when we recognize that beneath that failure in a complex and difficult art, may lie buried a sound legislator, an able architect, an original scientific investigator, or a good judge. Scientifically speaking, it is as unproven that there is any organic relation between the brain of the female and the production of art in the form of fiction, as that there is an organic relation between the hand of woman and the typewriter. Both the creative writer and the typist, in their respective spheres, are merely finding outlets for their powers in the direction of least mental resistance. The tendency of women at the present day to undertake certain forms of labor proves only that in the crabbed, walled-in, and bound conditions surrounding woman at the present day, these are the lines along which action is most possible to her.

It may possibly be that, in future ages, when the male and female forms have been placed in like intellectual conditions, with like stimuli, like trainings and like rewards, some aptitudes may be found running parallel with the line of sex function when humanity is viewed as a whole. It may possibly be that, when the historian of the future looks back over the history of the intellectually freed and active sexes for many generations, a decided preference of the female intellect for mathematics, engineering, or statecraft may be made clear; and that a like marked inclination in the male to excel in acting, music, or astronomy may by careful and large comparison be shown. But for the present, we have no adequate scien-

tific data from which to draw any con-
clusion, and any attempt to divide the
occupations in which male and female
intellects and wills should be employed,
must be to attempt a purely artificial
and arbitrary division: a division not
more rational and scientific than an attempt to determine by the color of his
eyes and the shape and strength of his
legs, whether a lad should be an astronomer or an engraver.

III

Those physical differences among mankind which divide races and nations—not merely those differences, enormously greater as they are generally, than any physical differences between male and female of the same race, which divide the Jew and the Swede, the Japanese and the Englishman, but even those subtle physical differences which divide closely allied races such as the English and German—often appear to be allied with subtle differences in intellectual aptitudes. Yet even with regard to these differences, it is almost impossible to determine scientifically in how far they are the result of national traditions, environment, and ed-

ucation, and in how far they run parallel with the differences in physical conformation.[1]

---

[1] In thinking of physical sex differences, the
civilized man of modern times has always to
guard himself against being unconsciously misled
by the very exaggerated external sex differences
which our unnatural method of sex clothing and
dressing the hair produces. The unclothed and
natural human male and female bodies are not
more divided from each other than those of the
lion and lioness. Our remote Saxon ancestors,
with their great white bodies and flowing hair
worn long by both sexes, were but little distin-
guished from each other; while among their modern descendants the short-haired, darkly clothed,
manifestly two-legged male differs absolutely
from the usually long-haired, color bedizened,
much skirted female. Were the structural differences between male and female really one-half as
marked as the artificial visual differences, they
would be greater than those dividing, not merely
any species of man from each other, but as great
as those which divide orders in the animal world.
Only a mind exceedingly alert and analytical can
fail ultimately to be misled by habitual visual mis-

No study of the mere physical differences between individuals of different races would have enabled us to arrive at any knowledge of their mental aptitude; nor does the fact that certain individuals of a given human variety have certain aptitudes form a rational ground for compelling all individuals of that variety to undertake a certain form of labor.

No analysis, however subtle, of the physical conformation of the Jew could have suggested *a priori,* and still less could have proved, apart from ages of practical experience, that, running par-

representation. There is not, probably, one man or woman in twenty thousand who is not powerfully influenced in modern life in their conception of the differences, physical and intellectual, dividing the human male and female, by the grotesque exaggerations of modern attire and artificial manners.

allel with any physical characteristics which may distinguish him from his fellows, was an innate and unique intellectual gift in the direction of religion. The fact that, during three thousand years, from Moses to Isaiah, through Jesus and Paul, on to Spinoza, the Jewish race has produced men who have given half the world its religious faith and impetus, proves that, somewhere and somehow, whether connected organically with that physical organization that marks the Jew, or as the result of his traditions and training, there does go this gift in the matter of religion. But, on the other hand, we find millions of Jews who are totally and markedly deficient in it, and to base any practical legislation for the individual even on this proven intellectual aptitude of the race as a whole

[29]

would be manifestly as ridiculous as abortive.

Yet more markedly, with the German—no consideration of his physical peculiarities, though it proceeded to the subtlest analysis of nerve, bone, and muscle, could in the present stage of our knowledge have proved to us what generations of experience appear to have proved, that, with that organization which constitutes the German, goes a unique aptitude for music. There is always the possibility of mistaking the result of training and external circumstance for inherent tendency, but when we consider the passion for music which the German has shown, and when we consider that the greatest musicians the world has seen, from Bach, Beethoven, and Mozart to Wagner, have been of that race, it appears highly

probable that such a correlation between the German organization and
the intellectual gift of music does exist.

Similar intellectual peculiarities
seem to be connoted by the external differences which mark off other races
from each other. Nevertheless, if per-
sons of all of these nationalities gathered in one colony, any attempt to legislate for their restriction to certain
forms of intellectual labor on the
ground of their apparently proved national aptitudes or disabilities, would
be regarded as insane. To insist that
all Jews, and none but Jews, should
lead and instruct in religious matters;
that all Englishmen, and none but Englishmen, should engage in trade; that
each German should make his living by
music, and none but a German allowed

to practice it, would drive to despair
the unfortunate individual Englishman, whose most marked deficiency
might be in the direction of finance and
bartering trade power; the Jew, whose
religious instincts might be entirely
rudimentary; or the German, who
could not distinguish one note from another; and the society as a whole would
be an irremediable loser, in one of the
heaviest of all forms of social loss—the
loss of the full use of the highest capacities of all its members.

IV

It may be that with sexes as with races, the subtlest physical differences between them may have their mental correlatives; but no abstract consideration of the human body in relation to its functions of sex can, in the present state of our knowledge, show us what intellectual capacities tend to vary with sexual structure, and nothing in the present or past condition of male or female gives us more than the very faintest possible indication of the relation of their intellectual aptitudes and their sexual functions. And even if it were proved by centuries of experiment that with the possession of the uterine function of sex tends to go exceptional intellectual capacity in the direction of mathematics rather than natural history, or an inclination for statecraft rather than for mechanical invention; were it proved that, generally speaking and as a whole, out of twenty thousand women devoting themselves to law and twenty thousand to medicine, they tended to achieve relatively more in the field of law than of medicine, there would yet be no possible healthy or rational ground for restricting the activities of the individual female to that line in which the average female appeared rather more frequently to excel.[1]

---

[1] Minds not keenly analytical are always apt to mistake mere correlation of appearance with causative sequence. We have heard it gravely asserted that between potatoes, pigs, mud cabins, and Irishmen there was an organic connection; but we who have lived in Colonies know that

That even one individual in a society should be debarred from undertaking that form of social toil for which it is most fitted, makes an unnecessary deficit in the general social assets. That one male Froebel should be prohibited or hampered in his labor as an educator of infancy, on the ground that infantile instruction was the field of the female; that one female with gifts in the direction of state administration, should be compelled to instruct an infants' school, perhaps without any gift for so doing, is a running to waste of social life-blood.

Free trade in labor and equality of

within two generations the pure-bred descendant of the mud cabin becomes often the successful politician, wealthy financier, or great judge; and shows no more predilection for potatoes, pigs, and mud cabins than men of any other race.

training, intellectual or physical, is essential if the organic aptitudes of a sex or class are to be determined. And our demand to-day is that natural conditions, inexorably, but beneficently, may determine the labors of each individual, and not artificial restrictions.

V

As there is no need to legislate that Hindus, being generally supposed to have a natural incapacity for field sports, shall not betake themselves to them—for, if they have no capacity, they will fail; and, as in spite of the Hindus' supposed general incapacity for sport, it is possible for an individual Hindu to become the noted batsman of his age; so, there is no need to legislate that woman should be restricted in her choice of fields of labor; for the organic incapacity of the individual, if it exist, will legislate far more strongly than any artificial, legal, or social obstruction can do; and it may be that the one individual in ten thousand who se-

[37]

lects a field not generally sought by his fellows will enrich humanity by the result of an especial genius. Allowing all to start from the one point in the world of intellectual culture and labor, with our ancient Mother Nature sitting as umpire, distributing the prizes and scratching from the lists the incompetent, is all we demand, but we demand it determinedly. Throw the puppy into the water: if it swims, well; if it sinks, well; but do not tie a rope round its throat and weight it with a brick, and then assert its incapacity to keep afloat.

For the present, *we take all labor for our province!*

From the judge's seat to the legislator's chair; from the statesman's closet to the merchant's office; from the chemist's laboratory to the astronomer's

tower, there is no post or form of toil
for which it is not our intention to attempt to fit ourselves; and there is no
closed door we do not intend to force
open; and there is no fruit in the gar-
den of knowledge it is not our determi-
nation to eat. Acting in us, and
through us, nature will mercilessly ex-
pose to us our deficiencies in the field
of human toil and reveal to us our powers. *And, for to-day, we take all labor
for our province!*

VI

But, it may be said: "What then of war, that struggle of the human creature to attain its ends by physical force and at the price of the life of others: will you take part in that also?" We reply: Yes; more particularly in that field we intend to play our part. We have always borne part of the weight of war, and the major part. It is not that in primitive times we suffered from the destruction of the fields we tilled and the houses we built; it is not that later as domestic laborers and producers, though unwaged, we, in taxes and material loss and additional labor, paid as much as our male towards the cost of war; it is not that in a comparatively insignificant manner, as nurses of the wounded in modern times, or now and again as warrior chieftainesses and leaders in primitive and other societies, we have borne our part; nor is it even because the spirit of resolution in its women, and their willingness to endure, has in all ages, again and again largely determined the fate of a race that goes to war, that we demand our controlling right where war is concerned. Our relation to war is far more intimate, personal, and indissoluble than this. Men have made boomerangs, bows, swords, or guns with which to destroy one another; we have made the men who destroyed and were destroyed! We have in all ages produced, at an enormous cost, the primal munition of war, without which no other would exist. There is no battlefield on earth, nor ever has been, howsoever covered with slain, which it has not cost the women of the race more in actual bloodshed and anguish to supply, than it has cost the men who lie there. *We pay the first cost on all human life.*

In supplying the men for the carnage of a battlefield, women have not merely lost actually more blood, and gone through a more acute anguish and weariness, in the long months of bearing and in the final agony of childbirth, than has been experienced by the men who cover it; but, in the long months of rearing that follow, the women of the race go through a long, patiently endured strain which no knapsacked soldier on his longest march has ever more than equaled; while, even in the matter of death, in all civilized societies, the probability that the average woman will die in child-birth is immeasurably greater than the probability that the average male will die in battle.

There is, perhaps, no woman, whether she have borne children, or be merely potentially a child-bearer, who could look down upon a battlefield covered with slain, but the thought would rise in her, "So many mothers' sons! So many young bodies brought into the world to lie there! So many months of weariness and pain while bones and muscles were shaped within! So many hours of anguish and struggle that breath might be! So many baby mouths drawing life at women's breasts;—all this, that men might lie with glazed eyeballs, and swollen faces, and fixed, blue, unclosed mouths, and

[43]

great limbs tossed—this, that an acre of ground might be manured with human flesh, that next year's grass or poppies or karoo bushes may spring up greener and redder, where they have lain, or that the sand of a plain may have a glint of white bones!" And we cry, "Without an inexorable cause, this must not be!" No woman who is a woman says of a human body, "It is nothing!"

VII

On that day when the woman takes her place beside the man in the governance and arrangement of external affairs of her race will also be that day that heralds the death of war as a means of arranging human differences. No tinsel of trumpets and flags will ultimately seduce women into the insanity of recklessly destroying life, or gild the willful taking of life with any other name than that of murder, whether it be the slaughter of the million or of one by one. And this will be, not because with the sexual function of maternity necessarily goes in the human creature a deeper moral insight, or a loftier type of social instinct than that which accompanies the paternal. Men have in all ages led as nobly as women in many paths of heroic virtue, and toward the higher social sympathies; in certain ages, being freer and more widely cultured, they have led further and better. The fact that woman has no inherent all-round moral superiority over her male companion, or naturally on all points any higher social instinct, is perhaps most clearly exemplified by one curious very small fact: the two terms signifying intimate human relationships, which in almost all human languages bear the most sinister and antisocial significance are both terms which have as their root the term "mother," and denote feminine relationships—the words "mother-in-law" and "step-mother."

In general humanity, in the sense of

social solidarity, and in magnanimity, the male has continually proved himself at least the equal of the female.

Nor will women shrink from war because they lack courage. Earth's women of every generation have faced suffering and death with an equanimity that no soldier on a battlefield has ever surpassed and few have equaled; and where war has been to preserve life, or land, or freedom, rather than for aggrandizement and power, unparasitized and laboring women have in all ages known how to bear an active part, and die.

Nor will woman's influence militate against war because in the future woman will not be able physically to bear her part in it. The smaller size of her muscle, which might severely have disadvantaged her when war was con-

[47]

ducted with a battle-axe or sword and hand to hand, would now little or not at all affect her. If intent on training for war, she might acquire the skill for guiding a Maxim or shooting down a foe with a Lee-Metford at four thousand yards as ably as any male; and undoubtedly, it has not been only the peasant girl of France, who has carried latent and hid in her person the gifts that would make the great general. If our European nations should continue in their present semi-civilized condition a few generations longer, it is highly probable that as financiers, as managers of the commissariat department, as inspectors of provisions and clothing for the army, women may probably play a very leading part; and that the nation which is the first to employ women may be placed at a vast ad-

[48]

vantage over its fellows in time of war. It is not because of woman's cowardice, incapacity, nor, above all, because of her general superior virtue, that she will end war when her voice is fully and clearly heard in the governance of states—it is because, on this one point, and on this point almost alone, the knowledge of woman, simply as woman, is superior to that of man; she knows the history of human flesh; she knows its cost; he does not.[1]

[1] It is noteworthy that even Catherine of Russia, a ruler and statesman of a virile and uncompromising type, and not usually troubled with moral scruples, yet refused with indignation the offer of Frederick of Prussia to pay her heavily for a small number of Russian recruits in an age when the hiring out of soldiers was common among the sovereigns of Europe.

VIII

In a besieged city, it might well happen that men in the streets might seize upon statues and marble carvings from public buildings and galleries and hurl them in to stop the breaches made in their ramparts by the enemy, unconsideringly and merely because they came first to hand, not valuing them more than had they been paving-stones. One man, however, could not do this—the sculptor. He, who, though there might be no work of his own chisel among them, yet knew what each of these works of art had cost, knew by experience the long years of struggle and study and the infinitude of toil which had gone to the shaping of even one

limb, to the carving of even one perfected outline, he could never so use
them without thought or care. Instinctively he would seek to throw in house-
hold goods, even gold and silver, all the
city held, before he sacrificed its works
of art!

Men's bodies are our woman's works
of art. Given to us power to control,
we will never carelessly throw them in
to fill up the gaps in human relationships made by international ambitions
and greeds. The thought would never
come to us as women, "Cast in men's
bodies; settle the thing so!" Arbitra-
tion and compensation would as naturally occur to us as cheaper and sim-
pler methods of bridging the gaps in
national relationships, as to the sculptor it would occur to throw in anything

rather than statuary, though he might be driven to that at last!

This is one of those phases of human life, not very numerous, but very important, toward which the man as man, and the woman as woman, on the mere ground of their different sexual function with regard to reproduction, stand, and must stand, at a somewhat differing angle. The physical creation of human life, which, in as far as the male is concerned, consists in a few moments of physical pleasure, to the female must always signify months of pressure and physical endurance, crowned with danger to life. To the male, the giving of life is a laugh; to the female, blood, anguish, and sometimes death. Here we touch one of the few yet important differences between man and woman as such.

[52]

The twenty thousand men prematurely slain on a field of battle, mean, to the women of their race, twenty thousand human creatures to be borne within them for months, given birth to in anguish, fed from their breasts and reared with toil, if the numbers of the tribe and the strength of the nation are to be maintained. In nations continually at war, incessant and unbroken child-bearing is by war imposed on all women if the state is to survive; and whenever war occurs, if numbers are to be maintained, there must be an increased child-bearing and rearing. This throws upon woman as woman a war tax, compared with which all that the male expends in military preparations is comparatively light.

The relations of the female toward the production of human life influence

[53]

undoubtedly even her relation toward animal and all life. "It is a fine day, let us go out and kill something!" cries the typical male of certain races, instinctively; "There is a living thing, it will die if it is not cared for," says the average woman, almost equally instinctively. It is true that the woman will sacrifice as mercilessly, as cruelly, the life of a hated rival or an enemy, as any male; *but she always knows what she is doing, and the value of the life she takes!* There is no light-hearted, careless enjoyment in the sacrifice of life to the normal woman; her instinct, instructed by experience, steps in to prevent it. She always knows what life costs; and that it is more easy to destroy than create it.

IX

It is also true, that, from the loftiest standpoint, the condemnation of war which has arisen in the human spirit, is in no sense related to any particular form of sex function. The man and the woman alike, who with Isaiah on the hills of Palestine, or the Indian Buddha under his bo-tree, have seen the essential unity of all sentient life; and who therefore see in war but a symptom of that crude discoördination of life on earth, not yet at one with itself, which affects humanity in these early stages of its growth; and who are compelled to regard as the ultimate goal of the race, though yet perhaps far distant across the ridges of innumerable coming ages, that harmony between all forms of conscious life, metaphorically prefigured by the ancient Hebrew, when he cried, "The wolf shall dwell with the lamb; and the leopard shall lie down with the kid; and the calf and the young lion and the fatling together, and a little child shall lead them!"— to the individual, whether man or woman, who has reached this standpoint, there is no need for enlightenment from the instincts of the childbearers of society as such; their condemnation of war, rising not so much from the fact that it is a wasteful destruction of human flesh, as that it is an indication of the non-existence of that coördination, the harmony which is summed up in the cry, "My little children, love one another."

But for the vast bulk of humanity,

probably for generations to come, the instinctive antagonism of the human child-bearer to reckless destruction of that which she has at so much cost produced will probably be necessary to educate the race to any clear conception of the bestiality and insanity of war.

X

War will pass when intellectual culture and activity have made possible to the female an equal share in the control and governance of modern national life; it will probably not pass away much sooner; its extinction will not be delayed much longer.

It is especially in the domain of war that we, the bearers of men's bodies, who supply its most valuable munition, who, not amid the clamor and ardor of battle, but singly, and alone, with a three-in-the-morning courage, shed our blood and face death that the battlefield might have its food, a food more precious to us than our heart's blood; it is we especially who, in the domain of war, have our word to say, a word no man can say for us. It is our intention to enter into the domain of war and to labor there till in the course of generations we have extinguished it.

If to-day we claim all labor for our province, yet more especially do we claim those fields in which the difference in the reproductive function between man and woman may place male and female at a slightly different angle with regard to certain facts of human life.

THE END

www.ingramcontent.com/pod-product-compliance
Lightning Source LLC
Chambersburg PA
CBHW022342280326
41934CB00006B/752